W9-BJD-236

21st Century Skills Library

REAL WORLD MATH: GEOGRAPHY

RIVERS

BY JOHN NESTOR

Published in the United States of America by
Cherry Lake Publishing, Ann Arbor, Michigan
www.cherrylakepublishing.com

Content Adviser

Andrew Dombard, Associate Professor, Department of Earth and Environmental
Sciences, University of Illinois at Chicago
Math Adviser: Tonya Walker, MA, Boston University

Credits

Photos: Cover and page 1, ©kavram, used under license from Shutterstock, Inc.;
page 4, ©Bob Gibbons/Alamy; page 7, ©Andy Katzung/Alamy; page 8, ©iStockphoto.
com/lucienvanlinden; page 10, ©iStockphoto.com/JonathanChambers; page 13,
©Andy Z., used under license from Shutterstock, Inc.; page 14, ©iStockphoto.com/
tomorrowspix; page 16, ©Gregory Bergman/Alamy; page 19, ©iofoto, used under
license from Shutterstock, Inc.; page 20, ©iStockphoto.com/karimhesham; page 22,
©blickwinkel/Alamy; page 25, ©Peter Crighton/Alamy; page 26, ©View Stock/Alamy

Library of Congress Cataloging-in-Publication Data

Nestor, John.
  Rivers / by John Nestor.
    p. cm.—(Real world math: geography)
  Includes index.
  ISBN-13: 978-1-60279-497-9
  ISBN-10: 1-60279-497-9
  1. Rivers—Juvenile literature. I. Title.
II. Series.
  GB1203.8.N47 2010
  551.48'3—dc22   2008048308

Cherry Lake Publishing would like to acknowledge
the work of The Partnership for 21st Century Skills.
Please visit *www.21stcenturyskills.org* for more information.

TABLE OF CONTENTS

CHAPTER ONE
WHAT ARE RIVERS?

Did you know that blood vessels are carrying oxygen through your body right now? Those blood vessels are feeding your muscles and organs. Rivers and streams do something similar. But they feed the land.

The source of the River Loue is a huge cave in Eastern France.

Can you guess how many miles of blood vessels your body has? Now guess how many miles of rivers and streams flow through the United States. Which number do you think is bigger?

Before we find out the answer, let's ask another question: What are rivers? Rivers are natural streams of water that flow into lakes or oceans. But rivers don't just magically appear.

REAL WORLD MATH CHALLENGE

A town's playing fields border a river. The town uses the river to water the playing fields. It takes 500 gallons (1,893 liters) to water the fields. The town workers must water the fields 3 times a week. **How much water would the town take from the river each week?** Let's say the fields need water only 31 weeks a year. **How many gallons would the town take out of the river in a year?**

(Turn to page 29 for the answers)

The place where a river begins is called its source. A river's source can be many things. It can be a melting **glacier** or a natural spring. Sometimes a river starts at a lake that over-flows. A river most often begins in high areas, such as hills or mountains. As the river runs downstream, it picks up water from other rivers and streams, and from falling rain or snow.

21ST CENTURY CONTENT

Early Native Americans used the Mississippi River for trade and travel. The Anishinabe people (Ojibwe Indians) called the river *Messipi* or *Mee-zee-see-bee*, which means "big river" or "father of waters." In 1541, Spanish explorer Hernando de Soto became the first European to discover the river. Many cities and towns have developed along the river since then. Today, the Mississippi River is one of the world's busiest waterways for business. Why do you think that's true?

For example, take one of North America's longest rivers. The Mississippi River starts at Lake Itasca in northern Minnesota. The lake sits 1,475 feet (450 meters) above sea level. The river flows south from there all the way to the Gulf of Mexico! The Mississippi River runs for 2,340 miles (3,766 kilometers).

Now, back to that question about the number of miles of blood vessels and rivers and streams. If you guessed the United States has more miles of rivers and streams than your body has blood vessels, you were right. A child's body has more than 60,000 miles (96,561 km) of blood vessels. The United States has about 3.5 million miles (5.6 million km) of rivers and streams.

Shipping barges are a common sight on the Mississippi River.

CHAPTER TWO
WHAT DO RIVERS DO?

Rivers are an important part of Earth's water system. They help to sculpt the landscape. They also carry huge amounts of water from the land to the sea. In some

The Grand Canyon is one of the most amazing landmarks in the United States.

places, the water also picks up polluted **runoff** from cities, industries, and farms.

The water at the source of a river is usually pure. As the water flows downstream, it picks up small pieces of soil or rock called **sediment**. A river's flowing water and sediment cause **erosion**. That's the gradual wearing away of the riverbank.

REAL WORLD MATH CHALLENGE

Donovan's Boy Scout troop is going on a camping trip in Florida. The troop will be taking a canoe trip down the Apalachicola River, which is 112 miles long. The last 30 miles of the river are surrounded by swamps. **If the troop begins their trip 42 miles from the river's starting point and stops canoeing when they reach the swamps, how far have they traveled? What percentage of the river is that?**

(Turn to page 29 for the answers)

Rivers erode land and carry it downstream toward the sea or lake it flows into. This kind of erosion can form deep valleys called **canyons** as well as waterfalls. For example, erosion created the massive Grand Canyon in Arizona and the enormous Victoria Falls in southern Africa.

The Grand Canyon was formed by the Colorado River. The Grand Canyon is 277 miles (446 km) long and more than 1 mile (1.6 km) deep in places. Only a portion of the Colorado flows through the Grand Canyon. The river measures about 1,450 miles (2,334 km) from where it starts in northern Colorado to where it empties in Southern California.

Niagara Falls is a popular tourist attraction for Canadians and Americans.

Victoria Falls was formed by the Zambezi River. The falls are 355 feet (108 m) high. That's about twice as high as Niagara Falls, which are waterfalls located on the border between the United States and Canada.

The end of a river, where it empties into a larger body of water, is called the **mouth**. A river **delta** is usually found there. A delta is a mass of sand and mud that collects at the mouth of a river. Deltas are often shaped in a triangle. They get their name from the Greek letter *delta*, which is shaped like a triangle.

LIFE & CAREER SKILLS

Many birds, fish, and mammals—such as otters, seals, and crabs—live in **estuaries**. People live, swim, fish, and bird-watch in estuaries and the areas around them. In fact, the U.S. Congress set up the National Estuary Program in 1987 to protect the country's important estuaries. All government agencies, as well as community members, business leaders, educators, and researchers, take part in the individual programs. They work hard to safeguard these centers of our coastal communities.

Another part of some rivers is called an estuary. That's the wide part of a river where the river's freshwater meets the salty sea or ocean water. Estuaries are often called bays, sounds, or harbors. Many of the world's largest cities are located on estuaries.

REAL WORLD MATH CHALLENGE

Did you know that salt water is heavier than freshwater? Seawater has about 35 gallons of salt for every 1,000 gallons of water. **What percentage of seawater is salt?**

(Turn to page 29 for the answer)

When a river flows into a sea or ocean at an estuary, the heavier salt water sinks and the lighter freshwater rises. This natural process helps keep the estuary waters clean and full of oxygen.

Many large cities, such as San Francisco, are located near estuaries because of their usefulness for water transportation.

CHAPTER THREE

DO THE MATH: NORTH AMERICAN RIVERS

Thousands of large and small rivers flow through North America. The United States alone has more than 250,000

Kansas City is just one city that is on the banks of the Missouri River.

rivers. If every state had the same number of rivers, then each would have 5,000 rivers!

The Missouri River is a **tributary** of the Mississippi River. That means it flows into the Mississippi. But the Missouri River is also the longest river in the United States. The Missouri starts in the Rocky Mountains of Montana. It runs for 2,540 miles (4,088 km) until it reaches the Mississippi River north of Saint Louis, Missouri.

After the Missouri, the Mississippi is the longest river in the United States. It is 2,340 miles (3,766 km) long. The mighty Mississippi is deeper than the Missouri, however.

REAL WORLD MATH CHALLENGE

The Missouri River is 2,540 miles long. The Mississippi is 2,340 miles long. The Yukon River is 1,980 miles. **How much longer is the Missouri River than the Mississippi and Yukon rivers? What percentage longer is it?**

(Turn to page 29 for the answers)

One of the longest rivers in North America is the Yukon. It flows for 1,980 miles (3,187 km) through Alaska and Canada's Yukon Territory. The Yukon River empties into the Bering Sea.

Other long North American rivers are the Rio Grande and the Saint Lawrence. They are both 1,900 miles (3,058 km) long. The Rio Grande starts in the Rocky Mountains of Colorado and empties into the Gulf of Mexico. The Saint Lawrence connects the Great Lakes with the Atlantic Ocean.

The Rio Grande River acts as a natural border between Mexico and the United States.

All of these great rivers have played a major role in the development of North America. Americans built most of the early settlements along these rivers for travel, transportation, and use as trade routes. In 1811, steamboats began traveling along the Mississippi River. This helped to make it one of the most important trade and travel routes in the country. Today, the Mississippi continues to be an important waterway for transporting goods. Every year, almost 500 million tons of cargo travel on the mighty Mississippi on giant barges.

Rivers also help provide the water we need to live. The Mississippi provides almost 18 million people with water for drinking, washing, and watering crops. People around the world depend on river water to meet their needs.

REAL WORLD MATH CHALLENGE

Nora, Amari, and Max took 2 weeks to collect water samples and record wildlife and plant sightings along the Farmington River **watershed**. (A watershed is the land that drains into a stream, river, or lake.) The watershed area is 609 square miles. The group covered 80% of it. **How much area of the watershed did they cover? How much did they cover on average every day during their 2 weeks?**

(Turn to page 29 for the answers)

Rivers can also be used to generate electricity. Hoover Dam is located on the Colorado River. It contains a hydroelectric power plant that provides energy for people in Nevada, Arizona, and California. Hydroelectric power plants provide nearly 20 percent of all the electricity used today.

The Hoover Dam supplies electricity to towns throughout Nevada, California, and Arizona.

CHAPTER FOUR
DO THE MATH: THE NILE AND AMAZON

North America is home to many rivers, but it is not home to the longest. That honor belongs to Africa, where the Nile River is found. The Nile River flows

Throughout history, many civilizations have been built along the banks of the Nile.

4,132 miles (6,650 km) from its source to its mouth. It gets its name from the Greek word *nelios*, which means "river valley."

The Nile and its tributaries flow though nine countries in Africa. The Nile is formed from two rivers. The White Nile starts at Lake Victoria in central Africa. The source of the Blue Nile is Ethiopia's Lake Tana. These rivers meet in Sudan and then flow northward, toward the Mediterranean Sea.

21ST CENTURY CONTENT

The Nile is officially the longest river in the world. Scientists have argued about this for a very long time, though. Many South American scientists believe that the Amazon is the longest river. It is very difficult to figure out the exact length of a river. Rivers are always connected to other bodies of water. This makes it hard for scientists to decide where the river starts and ends. The debate about which river is longer continues today.

There are many types of wildlife in and along the Nile River. More than 100 different species of fish swim in the waters of the Nile. Falcons, owls, parrots, and many other kinds of birds fly in the skies above the river. Hungry eagles dive down and snatch their prey from the water. Many animals also live on the land that surrounds the river. Elephants, hippopotamuses, and giraffes are just three of the animals that use the Nile for drinking and bathing. The Nile is also well known for its population of crocodiles.

Elephants play in the cool waters of the Nile.

The Amazon River in South America is almost as long as the Nile. It is the world's second-longest river at 4,000 miles (6,437 km). While it is not the longest, this river is certainly the widest—7 miles (11 km) in some points. When the Amazon floods during the rainy season, it can be nearly 30 miles (48 km) wide!

REAL WORLD MATH CHALLENGE

Elad is measuring the length of a river on a map. Each inch on his map equals 200 miles. **How many miles is the river if Elad measures 4 inches on the map? If the river is 1,000 miles long, how many inches would it be on his map?**

(Turn to page 29 for the answers)

The Amazon is the river that carries the most water. It accounts for about 20 percent of all the water that the world's rivers pour into the oceans. The Amazon collects water from 40 percent of the South American continent. It has thousands of tributaries, many of which are more than 1,000 miles (1,609 km) long.

The Amazon River isn't amazing just for its size. It is part of the Amazon rain forest ecosystem. This rain forest contains almost 80,000 species of trees and 55,000 species of flowers.

Most of these plants can't be found anywhere else on Earth. In some places, the plant growth is so thick that sunlight can't reach the rain forest floor.

REAL WORLD MATH CHALLENGE

The Amazon is one of the world's most famous rivers. It produces about 20% of all the water that the world's rivers pour into the oceans. **If the world's rivers pour 3.5 million gallons of water into the oceans each day, how much does the Amazon pour in each day?**

(Turn to page 29 for the answer)

This dense plant growth is home to an unbelievable variety of animal life. About 10 percent of all the animals in the world live in the Amazon. There are hundreds of mammal species and thousands of fish species. There are so many different kinds of insects and spiders that no one has been able to figure out the exact number. Some scientists believe there could be as many as 60 million species!

The Amazon and its tributaries run through tropical rain forests.

CHAPTER FIVE
OTHER GREAT RIVERS OF THE WORLD

Rivers are located on six of the seven continents. Only Antarctica has no rivers. Can you guess why? Rivers cannot flow because ice covers almost entirely this frozen continent.

The water of the Yangtze River is muddy in many areas.

Let's take a look at the longest rivers on the other six continents. We've already talked about the Nile, which flows for 4,132 miles (6,650 km). Besides being the world's longest river, it's also Africa's longest river. And we talked about the Amazon, the world's second-longest river. It's also the longest river in South America, at 4,000 miles (6,437 km). Asia's longest river is the Yangtze. It stretches 3,434 miles (5,526 km) into the East China Sea.

REAL WORLD MATH CHALLENGE

Land covers about 29% of Earth's surface. Earth's total surface area is about 197,000,000 square miles. **What percentage of Earth's surface is water? How many square miles of water are there?**

(Turn to page 29 for the answers)

Do you remember the longest river in North America? That's the Missouri River, at 2,540 miles (4,088 km). The longest river in Europe is the Volga. It flows into the Caspian Sea after 2,193 miles (3,529 km). Finally, Australia's longest river is the Darling River. It's 1,702 miles (2,739 km) long.

Water covers much of Earth's surface. Think of all the oceans, seas, lakes, rivers, and streams in the world. Now guess how much of Earth's surface is covered by water.

The answer is nearly three-fourths. But there is not as much water for us to use as you might think. Only about 1 percent of water on Earth is available for humans to use. That's because most of Earth's water is salt water. Only 3 percent of Earth's water is freshwater. And two-thirds of the world's freshwater is frozen in glaciers and polar ice. That leaves just 1 percent, a large portion of which is the water found in rivers. Just how important are rivers? With numbers like these, the answer is clear. We need rivers to survive!

LEARNING & INNOVATION SKILLS

Earth's population increases every year. The amount of water on Earth never changes, though. This means that we need to think about new ways to conserve water. About 70 percent of our freshwater supply is used for farming. What are some ways farmers could use less water and still grow enough food for everyone?

People also use a lot of water in their everyday lives. What are some ways you and your family could help conserve water? With enough good ideas, there will be plenty of water for everyone in the future.

REAL WORLD MATH CHALLENGE ANSWERS

Chapter One

Page 5

The town takes 1,500 gallons a week from the river.
3 times a week x 500 gallons = 1,500 gallons
The town takes 46,500 gallons of water from the river each year to water the fields.
31 weeks x 1,500 gallons = 46,500 gallons

Chapter Two

Page 9

The troop canoed 40 miles.
112 miles – 42 miles – 30 miles = 40 miles
The troop canoed down 36% of the river.
40 ÷ 112 = 0.357 0.357 = 36%

Page 12

3.5% of seawater is salt.
35 gallons ÷ 1,000 gallons = 0.035
0.035 = 3.5%

Chapter Three

Page 15

The Missouri River is 200 miles longer than the Mississippi. That's 8% longer.
2,540 miles – 2,340 miles = 200 miles
200 miles ÷ 2,540 miles = 0.078 = 8%
The Missouri is 560 miles longer than the Yukon. That's 22% longer.
2,540 miles – 1,980 miles = 560 miles
560 miles ÷ 2,540 miles = 0.22 = 22%

Page 18

If they covered 80% of 609 square miles, they covered 487.2 square miles.
80% = .80
.80 x 609 square miles = 487.2 square miles
Over the 14 days (2 weeks), they covered an average of 34.8 square miles a day.
487.2 square miles ÷ 14 days = 34.8 square miles a day

Chapter Four

Page 23

The river is 800 miles long.
4 inches x 200 miles = 800 miles
The river would measure 5 inches on the map.
1,000 miles ÷ 200 miles = 5 inches

Page 24

The Amazon pours 700,000 gallons of water into the oceans each day.
20% = .20
3,500,000 gallons x .20 = 700,000 gallons each day

Chapter Five

Page 27

71% of Earth's surface is water.
100% – 29% = 71%
Earth has 139,870,000 square miles of water.
197,000,000 square miles x 71% (or .71) = 139,870,000 square miles

GLOSSARY

canyons (KAN-yuhnz) deep valleys formed by running water

delta (DEL-tuh) a mass of sand and mud, often shaped like a triangle, that collects at the mouth of a river

erosion (i-ROH-zhuhn) the gradual wearing away of something, caused by water or wind

estuaries (ESS-chu-er-reez) coastal areas where freshwater from rivers and streams mixes with salt water from the ocean

glacier (GLAY-shur) a huge ice sheet moving slowly down a mountain or valley

mouth (MOUTH) the end of a river, where it empties into a larger body of water

runoff (RUHN-awf) rainwater that is not absorbed by the ground and ends up in streams and rivers

sediment (SED-uh-muhnt) small pieces of soil or rocks that are carried by water, wind, or glaciers

tributary (TRIB-yuh-ter-ee) a river or stream that flows into a larger stream, river, or lake

watershed (WAW-tur-shed) the land that drains into a stream, river, or lake

FOR MORE INFORMATION

BOOKS

Banting, Erinn. *The Nile River: The Longest River in the World*. New York: Weigl Publishers, 2004.

Graf, Mike. *The Amazon River*. Mankato, MN: Capstone Press, 2006.

Telford, Carole, and Rod Theodorou. *Down a River*. Chicago: Heinemann, 2006.

WEB SITES

American Rivers—River Basics: River Facts
www.americanrivers.org/site/PageServer?pagename=AR7_RiverFacts
A collection of interesting facts about rivers

National Wild and Scenic Rivers System—Rivers and Kids
www.rivers.gov/kids/index.html
Read about wild and scenic rivers in the United States

River World
www.kented.org.uk/ngfl/subjects/geography/rivers/
Links to river photos and more information about river features

INDEX

ABOUT THE AUTHOR

John Nestor has been a writer and editor for more than 15 years. He has had the pleasure of writing about subjects ranging from ducklings hatching in a second grade classroom to Tiger Woods winning The Masters.

John lives in northwest Connecticut with his wife Nancy and their three children James, Jack, and Samantha.